Man's Best Friend

A Guide to Understanding and Loving Your Dog

Dr. Kyle Williams

Table of Content

Contents

Introduction

Once upon a time, there lived a man and his faithful companion, a loyal canine. From the moment they met, the man and his dog had an unbreakable connection.

The man and his dog went everywhere together. They took long walks in the park, went on camping trips, and even spent time just cuddling on the couch. The man was so proud of his canine companion, and the canine was just as proud of his human companion.

The man was determined to make his canine companion the happiest pup in the world, so he studied everything he could about taking care of a dog. He learned about proper nutrition, exercise, grooming, and playtime. He also became an expert on canine behaviour, learning how to read his pet's body language and understand what he was trying to tell him.

With the man's knowledge, two were unstoppable. The man and his dog were rarely apart and shared an unbreakable bond. The man was so proud of his canine companion, and the canine was just as proud of his human companion.

The two were best friends, and the man was always glad to have such a loyal and loving companion by his side. He knew that no matter what, his canine friend would always be there for him, and that was all that mattered.

The man had finally found his best friend, and with his knowledge, he could provide the canine companion with the best possible life. He was sure that his canine friend would remain faithful and loving to him for years to come.

The man and his canine friend could not be separated, and they lived happily ever after.

Man's Best Friend – A Guide to Understanding and Loving Your Dog is a comprehensive guide to the wonderful world of pet ownership. Whether you are a first-time dog owner or a seasoned veteran, this book will give you the insight and understanding to build a strong and lasting bond with your canine companion. You will learn how to interpret your dog's behaviour, how to keep them healthy, and how to make sure they are getting the best care possible. You can also look forward to a deep dive into your dog's habits, needs, and emotions, and how to properly care for them in various situations. From the basics of house training to advanced obedience training, you will have the answers to the questions that you have been longing to ask. This book will be the perfect companion to help you understand and love your dog even more.

With Man's Best Friend – A Guide to Understanding and Loving Your Dog, you will come away with a newfound appreciation for the four-legged friends that have been loyal companions for centuries. It is sure to be the perfect resource for any dog owner.

Chapter One

The History of Man's Best Friend

The history of the beloved canine companion goes back thousands of years. Dogs evolved from ancient wolves and were domesticated by humans as early as 12,000 years ago. Scientists believe that man and wolf began to form a relationship when humans started to hunt in packs and needed help tracking prey.

Over the centuries, people have bred and trained dogs for a variety of purposes, from protection to hunting to companionship. Dogs have been used to herd sheep, pull sleds and carts, and even assist in military operations.

Today, dogs are primarily kept as pets. They are beloved companions and are often considered members of the family. People have bred dogs to bring out certain characteristics, from size and shape to behavior and coat color. As a result, there is a wide variety of breeds that can fit into any lifestyle.

The bond between humans and dogs is truly special, and it's easy to see why these loyal companions are known as "man's best friend."

It's impossible to know the exact history of man's best friend, but one thing is for certain—dogs have been by our side for centuries and will continue to be our faithful friends for many years to come.

Chapter Two

Choosing the Right Dog

When it comes to choosing the right dog for your family, there are many factors to consider. First, you should determine what kind of lifestyle you have, as this will help you decide which breed is best suited to your family. Additionally, you should research the different breeds and their temperaments, as this can help you narrow down your search even further.

Second, you should consider the size of your home, as larger breeds may be too much for small spaces. Third, you should think about your family's activity level and energy level. If your family is very active, you may want to look for a breed that can keep up with them. On the other hand, if your family is more laid-back, then you may want to look for a calmer breed.

Finally, you should consider the cost of caring for a dog. Feeding, grooming, and veterinary care can add up quickly, so it's important to consider this before making a decision.

Choosing the right dog isn't a decision to be taken lightly. By taking the time to research the different breeds and consider your lifestyle, you can make sure you're bringing home a canine companion that's right for you and your family.

Chapter Three

Bonding with Your Dog

Can be a fun and rewarding experience for both you and your pet. It is important to remember that the bond between you and your pet will take time, effort, and patience to develop.

The best way to start bonding with your dog is by spending quality time together. Walks, playtime, and training sessions are all great ways to get to know your pet and build trust between you. When you are interacting with your dog, make sure to provide positive reinforcement like praises and treats when they do something right. This will help them to create a positive association with you and help build a bond between you.

It is also important to establish a routine for your dog. This helps them to feel secure and provides structure to their days. Having a consistent feeding schedule, playtime, and training sessions will help create a sense of security and trust between you and your pet.

Finally, make sure to provide your pet with plenty of love and affection. Show them that you care by petting them, brushing them, and playing with them. This is a great way to show your pet that you care about them and will help strengthen the bond between the two of you.

Bonding with your dog is a process that takes time, effort, and patience. However, the rewards of having a strong and trusting bond with your pet are worth it. By taking the time to build a strong relationship with your pet, you will be able to enjoy a long and happy life together

Chapter Four

Training and Obedience

Training and obedience are essential in creating a successful and happy relationship between people and their pets. Training allows you to create a healthy and balanced lifestyle for your pet and establish a more harmonious relationship between you and your pet. Obedience is also an important part of training as it allows you to communicate with your pet and teach it how to respond to commands.

Training and obedience should be consistent, positive, and reward-based, not punitive. This means that you should reward your pet for good behaviour and discourage bad behaviour. Positive reinforcement is an effective way to train your pet and can help build trust and loyalty. Training should be fun for both you and your pet and should be tailored to your pet's individual needs.

When it comes to obedience, teaching your pet simple commands such as sit, stay, and come is a great way to start. You can also teach your pet more complex commands such as fetch, roll over, and drop it. As your pet learns these commands, you can increase the difficulty and reward your pet for obeying.

Training and obedience are important in creating a bond between you and your pet.

With consistent, positive reinforcement, you can create a healthy and happy relationship that will last a lifetime

Chapter Five

Grooming and Health Care

Grooming and health care are two essential aspects of any pet's life. By taking the time to properly groom and care for your pet, you can help to keep them healthy and happy. Grooming involves brushing, bathing, and trimming fur and nails, as well as inspecting your pet for any potential problems or illnesses. Health care is the proactive approach to keeping your pet in good health and includes regular vet visits and vaccinations, as well as making sure your pet is eating the right food and getting enough exercise.

Brushing your pet's fur regularly is important for getting rid of dead fur and removing any dirt or debris. This helps to keep their coat looking its best and can also help to reduce shedding. When bathing your pet, it's important to use a gentle shampoo that is specifically designed for pets. Trimming your pet's nails should also be done regularly to help keep them at a safe length and prevent any painful scratches.

Health care for your pet should include regular visits to the vet to make sure they are up-to-date on their vaccinations and check-ups. It's also important to make sure your pet is eating a healthy diet and getting enough exercise. Exercise helps to keep your pet's muscles and joints healthy and can also help to reduce stress.

By taking the time to properly groom and care for your pet, you can help to keep them healthy and happy. Grooming and health care are important for any pet and can help to ensure that your pet lives a long and healthy life

Chapter Six

Finding the Right Vet.

Finding the right vet for your pet can be a difficult process. You want to find someone who is knowledgeable, experienced, and caring. Here are some tips to help you in your search:

1. Get referrals. Ask friends, family, or your current vet for recommendations. You can also consult online reviews and directories to find local veterinary clinics.
2. Research the veterinarians. Look into the veterinarians' credentials, experience, and specializations. Check

to make sure they are board certified and accredited by the American Veterinary Medical Association.

3. Visit the clinic. Make an appointment to visit the clinic and meet the vet. This is a great opportunity to ask questions and get a feel for the clinic.
4. Consider your pet's needs. Do you need a vet who specializes in a particular species or breed? Do you need a vet who offers additional services such as grooming or nutrition counselling?
5. Ask questions. When you meet the vet, make sure to ask about their experience, techniques, and philosophies. Ask about the clinic's policies and fees.

Finding the right vet for your pet is an important decision. Take your time and do your research to make sure you find the best vet for your pet's needs.

Chapter Seven

Traveling with Your Dog

To explore the world together, traveling with your dog can be a great way to bond. However, it is important to ensure that you are doing everything you can to keep your pup safe and comfortable during your journey. Here are a few tips for making your next trip with your furry friend a success:

1. Research ahead of time: Make sure to research the area you are traveling to and the rules and regulations concerning traveling with a pet. This will

help you plan ahead and know what to expect during your travels.

2. Pack the essentials: Make sure to pack the necessary items for your pup, like food, water, treats, toys, a collar, leash, and waste bags. It's also a good idea to bring a first-aid kit and any necessary medications.
3. Take breaks: When traveling, you should take regular breaks to allow your dog to move around, have a bathroom break, and get a drink of water. This will help prevent your pup from getting too tired and uncomfortable during the journey.
4. Make sure your pet is comfortable: If you're driving, make sure your pup has

a comfortable spot to sit or lay down. If you're flying, check with the airline to make sure your pet is allowed in the cabin with you.

Traveling with your pup can be a fun and rewarding experience, but it's important to take the necessary precautions to ensure your pet's safety and comfort. With the right planning and preparation, you'll be sure to have a great time exploring with your furry friend!

Chapter Eight

Dealing with Behavioural Issues

Behavioural issues need to be addressed in a proactive, positive manner. The goal is to provide the necessary support and guidance to help the individual manage their behaviour, while also teaching them the skills to prevent future issues from arising.

First and foremost, it is important to understand what is causing the behaviour. This can be done through assessment and open communication. Once the underlying cause is identified, it is important to create a plan that can help the individual learn the skills needed to manage their behaviour. This plan should focus on positive reinforcement and incentives, as well as providing guidance and support.

It is also important to be consistent and patient when dealing with behavioural issues. This means providing clear and consistent consequences for the behaviour, as well as offering positive reinforcement and support. Additionally, it is important to recognize and acknowledge successes and progress, no matter how small.

Finally, it is important to create an environment of trust and respect. This means taking time to listen and learn from the individual, as well as being open to feedback and input from them.

By creating a safe and supportive environment, the individual can feel more comfortable expressing their needs and feelings, which can help to reduce the risk of future behaviour issues.

Overall, dealing with behavioural issues can be a challenging, but rewarding experience. By understanding the underlying cause, creating a positive plan of action, and maintaining consistency and respect, it is possible to help the individual manage their behaviour and prevent future issues from arising.

Chapter Nine

Nutrition and Exercise

Nutrition and exercise are two of the most important elements of leading a healthy and balanced lifestyle. Eating a balanced diet and getting regular physical activity are key components to improving overall health and wellness. Eating a healthy and balanced diet provides the body with essential nutrients, vitamins, and minerals that are needed for proper growth and development. Eating a variety of foods from all the food groups helps to ensure that you are getting enough vitamins and minerals in your diet. At the same time, physical activity is important for maintaining a healthy weight, reducing stress, and improving overall physical and mental health. Exercise can also help to reduce the risk of certain diseases, such as heart disease and type 2 diabetes.

To get the most out of a healthy lifestyle, it is important to find a balance between nutrition and exercise. A well-rounded diet should include plenty of fruits, vegetables, whole grains, lean proteins, and healthy fats. Eating a variety of different foods helps to ensure that you are getting all the essential nutrients and vitamins your body needs. Exercise, on the other hand, helps to burn calories, build muscle, and improve cardiovascular health. The best way to get the most out of your exercise routine is to find an activity that you enjoy and that fits into your lifestyle

By combining a healthy diet and regular physical activity, you can achieve optimal health and wellness. Eating a balanced diet and getting regular physical activity can help to reduce your risk of chronic diseases and improve your overall health and well-being. Eating a variety of foods from all the food groups and including regular physical activity into your daily routine are the best way to ensure that you are getting the nutrition and exercise your body needs.

Chapter Ten

Aging and End of Life Care.

Aging and end-of-life care are two topics that can be difficult to discuss but are essential to understand to ensure that everyone's wishes are respected and that they are provided with the best possible care. As people age, they face a variety of physical, emotional, and cognitive changes that can significantly affect their ability to care for themselves and make decisions. End of life care is a unique set of services and treatment options that are tailored to meet the individual's needs and wishes, and to ensure that they receive the highest quality of care during the final stages of life.

Aging and end of life care involve a wide range of topics, including understanding the physical, emotional, and cognitive changes associated with aging, recognizing the signs and symptoms of end-stage diseases and conditions, determining the best course of action for a particular situation, and managing pain and other symptoms. It is important to understand the various treatment options and services available for those facing end of life care, as well as what types of support are available for families and caregivers.

When considering end of life care, it is important to consider the individual's wishes and preferences regarding their care. This includes topics such as advance directives or living wills, palliative care, and hospice care. The goal is to make sure that the individual's wishes are respected and that they receive the best possible care for the remainder of their life.

It is also important to be aware of the various legal, financial, and ethical considerations that may arise when dealing with aging and end of life care. This includes topics such as estate planning, legal guardianship, and end of life decisions. It is important to be aware of these considerations and to make sure that the individual's wishes are respected.

Aging and end of life care can be difficult topics to discuss, but they are essential to ensure that everyone’s wishes are respected and that they are provided with the best possible care. It is important to be aware of the various topics and considerations associated with aging and end of life care, and to make sure that the individual’s wishes are respected.

Conclusion

Dogs have been our faithful companions for thousands of years and the bond between us has only grown stronger. Dogs are often called "man's best friend" because of their loyalty and unconditional love. They provide us with companionship, unconditional love, and protection. Dogs can also help us to stay physically active, reduce stress, and even help us to build relationships with other people. Dogs are truly amazing creatures and deserve our love and respect.

In conclusion, the bond between humans and dogs is special and unique. Dogs are hardworking, loyal, and loving animals that bring joy and companionship to our lives. They are truly man's best friend!

www.ingramcontent.com/pod-product-compliance
Lightning Source LLC
LaVergne TN
LVHW010510160826
845677LV00012B/2778